We The Peo

Written by Chodyna
Illustrated by Joshua Wichterich

We The People

ISBN: 978-1-7333944-0-6

Printed in the United States of America
First Trini-C LLC Edition, 2022

This book is dedicated to my beloved son, Mikey,

who served this nation with honors

in the U.S. Coast Guard.

Hey there children,
time to learn something true,
A lesson from We The People
has been written for you.

George Washington would kneel
as America began,
And to Almighty God,
he would dedicate this land.

The Founding Fathers were loyalists,
dedicated to the crown,
A land not born of rebellion,
but of honor and to be renown.

The founders that had come here
would soon find the crown to crush,
With over taxing policies
while their voices would be hushed.

Seen as petty folks across the pond,
with no voice to represent them,
Brought about a social unrest
that was cause for their dissension.

So they saw that a Monarchy
is very, very sad,
But also that a Democracy
would be very, very bad.

A Monarchy allows
one king to make the rules,
But a Democracy would be
run by a mob of fools.

The majority is a mob
of only fifty-one percent,
Which tells the other forty-nine
on what takes precedent.

So if the fifty-one would say,
"No ice cream", is their choice,
The forty-nine percent would lose
the power of their voice.

But if the minority had a law
to point to in defense,
Then ice cream can't be taken,
the law would hold prevalence.

We will have to make another way,
the Founding Fathers said,
A way where all society
will be protected.

An electoral college is good
to keep you from liberal harm,
For they'll always get the popular vote
when they're giving away the farm.

But freebies only bring about
division between the classes,
For virtue and wisdom never flow
when dealing with the masses.

Just think of two wolves and a lamb
that are voting what's for dinner,
But how dangerous the vote would be
when the lamb can't be the winner.

A Democracy looks like that,
a Monarchy won't work either,
So the Founding Fathers decided
that they would have to choose neither.

A system would be created,
correcting problems would be done,
The Constitutional Republic arose;
an experiment begun.

Not a government of men,
such as king or majority,
But a nation of We The People,
with laws as authority.

Yet a Constitutional Republic
won't work as it should,
Lest safeguards preserve liberty
and the laws that are made are good.

Still if the citizenry
have no respect for the law,
Anarchy surely ensues
and becomes our greatest flaw.

The only way to stop this
is with Freedom of Religion,
Fear of an ultimate God
must become public decision.

The moment we forget God
we are already in death,
We are simply waiting on
that one and final breath.

The Founding Fathers knew
a dictatorship would follow,
If the church no longer gathered,
Liberty's bell would ring hollow.

James Madison foresaw
a nation dividing into factions,
Balance of power would be needed
to stop majority taking actions.

If Senate, House, and Presidency
of same party gained all trust,
Then entire other factions
would get left behind in dust.

All factions, or parties,
must have their voices heard,
Or a lawless and fearless people
would silence opposing word.

The Bill of Rights was brought about
by fear of majority rule,
Something paramount to the Ten Commandments
would now harness the fool.

The Founding Fathers therefore said
Congress shall make no laws,
We must protect America from herself,
and that without clause.

No involvement in the diminishing
of the church of God allowed,
Preserving liberty,
enshrined and defended, adamantly vowed.

This 1st Amendment preserves our rights
like pickles in a jar,
The 2nd one is like it,
keeping government from reaching too far.

They cannot take our weapons,
our guns are here to stay,
For they knew a tyrannical government
would fall in future day.

In the Declaration of Independence
Thomas Jefferson would sight,
Life, Liberty, and pursuit of happiness
is the people's right.

And if the government established
is nothing but a hack,
Then it's the right of We The People
to take America back!

Made in the USA
Columbia, SC
27 September 2022